Materials Recycling: The Virtue of Necessity

William U. Chandler

Worldwatch Paper 56
October 1983

Library of Congress Catalog Card Number 83-51109
ISBN 0-916468-55-0

Printed on recycled paper

Table of Contents

Epimetheus, Prometheus' younger brother, precipitated the world's first materials crisis. Charged with allocating the earth's resources to its creatures, he gave wings to some, shells to others, but was so recklessly extravagant that he ran out before he came to human beings. Prometheus solved the crisis by stealing fire from the sun and giving it to mankind. With energy, the ultimate resource, humans could forever fashion tools and shelter from the abundant elements in the earth.[1]

The essential truth of the Promethean myth conveys both great hope and concern for sustaining human society. Energy transforms the earth's most common elements into materials humans can use. Trees use sunlight to produce wood virtually from thin air; 93 percent of the weight of the great mass of a tree comes from carbon dioxide taken from the atmosphere.[2] Society similarly applies energy to process ubiquitous minerals. Silicon, aluminum, and iron compose 40 percent of the earth's crust, and from them mankind bakes bricks and ceramics, blows glass, and refines pure metals. Iron and aluminum, in fact, constitute 94 percent of the metals used today.[3]

Wood, iron, and aluminum are now among mankind's most important materials, and they will be the basis of a sustainable future. But the future availability of these basic building blocks is clouded by the uncertain future of energy, a resource with painfully obvious constraints.[4] Simply maintaining current levels of materials production will require prodigious quantities of energy. World steel production alone consumes as much energy annually as Saudi Arabia produces. To increase worldwide per capita use of metals to U.S. levels would require the energy output of seven Saudi Arabias, or 40 percent of current total world commercial energy consumption. Many people still lack basic material amenities—metal for water pipes, wood for housing—and the world population is still growing. Recycling, fortunately, can cut the energy required in materials production by 50 to 90 percent, and thus help narrow the widening inequity between the world's rich and poor.

I would like to thank Hershel Cutler, Derrel DePasse, J. Rodney Edwards, Holly L. Gwin, and Ross Pumfrey for reviewing the manuscript, Sandie Nelson for advice, and Susan Hill for assistance in preparing this publication.

Throwing away an aluminum beverage container wastes as much energy as pouring out a can half-filled with gasoline.[5] Failing to recycle a daily edition of the *Washington Post* or *London Times* wastes just as much. Because the production and consumption of energy in wood, aluminum, and steel processing create severe environmental problems, environmental protection requires recycling.

Recycling also offers a substantial reduction in the cost of waste disposal. The economic burden and the political difficulty of expanding city dumps frequently prompt communities to turn to recycling. Solid waste disposal costs $30 to $100 per ton and represents a major budget item for many cities.[6] Residents often react strongly against having dumps located near their homes. The prospect of achieving a 40 percent reduction in solid waste, as some cities have done, presents leaders with a tangible political and economic opportunity.

Recycling thus saves energy and expensive raw materials, protects the environment, and cuts waste disposal costs. Despite these advantages, only about one-quarter of the world's paper, aluminum, or steel is recovered for reuse. Nevertheless, certain countries have made remarkable progress, and this progress has been promoted by common factors. Areas with high energy costs, scarce raw materials, and a strong desire to protect the environment have performed best in recycling. These cities, states, and countries have developed markets for the waste products they collect, and they have facilitated collection in a wide variety of ways. Many countries have invested in recycling equipment even when locally available scrap has been insufficient to satisfy demand. They have imported waste paper, scrap iron, and aluminum scrap and so have contributed to recycling elsewhere. Their investments have saved capital and energy and have improved their ability to compete in international markets by reducing debt, improving trade balances, and reducing the cost of their paper, iron, and aluminum. A large international trade in recyclable materials has developed, in fact, providing a powerful new tool that can be used to transform a wasteful world materials industry into one that is sustainable.

"Throwing away an aluminum beverage container wastes as much energy as pouring out a can half-filled with gasoline."

7

Society is much like a tree that may fabricate abundance from "thin air" but remains absolutely dependent upon small quantities of nutrients taken from the soil. A French journal recently asserted, "For industrial society, manganese and vanadium are more precious than gold," and warned that modern civilization would be impossible without exotic metals.[7] Chromium, manganese, magnesium, cobalt, and platinum are to society what nitrogen, phosphorus, potassium, and sulfur are to the green plant: strategic materials. Chromium hardens steel and protects it from rust. Cobalt provides strength and high temperature endurance to turbine blades and electromagnets. Magnesium strengthens aluminum.[8] Exotic metals by definition do not exist in abundance in the earth's crust and are not used in huge quantities. Except for copper and lead, industry recycles very small percentages of these materials. Technologies for recovering exotic metals are slowly developing, however, and will be increasingly applied. Because chromium, manganese, magnesium, and copper frequently serve as alloys, they can be recycled in concert with the base metals iron and steel and aluminum. Precious metals need to be recycled more efficiently as they become scarcer and more expensive, or replaced by more abundant substitutes. In this context, the Promethean myth is reassuring. Materials may be recycled or processed from low-grade ores as long as energy is sufficiently available and affordable. And even if the exotic metals must be processed from very low grade ores, the quantity of energy required should always be manageably small.[9]

Iron, aluminum, and wood take priority in recycling because their production requires prodigious quantities of energy and causes major environmental problems. Also, their abundance should satisfy demand for base materials in the foreseeable future. Among resources, however, wood takes a special place. Wood is both a fuel and building material. It is the raw material for paper. It will replace oil as a feedstock for chemicals production. And it is renewable. Sustaining the world's forests, already being depleted faster than they are being renewed, is a special necessity. Yet progress in recycling paper has been nowhere near as dramatic as in aluminum, and the paper recycling industry does not even approach in size that of iron and steel. Each material requires different recycling technologies, policies, and markets. The constraints on recycling may differ from resource to resource as much as trade barriers for iron scrap differ from tax subsidies for timber harvesting. The resolution of constraints may require action on planes as different as local zoning boards and international trade commissions. Each resource, its potential for recycling and its special technical and political circumstances, must be considered in turn.

The Virtue of Necessity

Recycling has been an environmental goal for a decade now, but only a few areas of the world have made significant progress. Voluntary recycling efforts have brought some success, but progress has come about mainly in response to necessity. Countries that have increased materials recycling have been motivated by three main factors: short supply of raw materials, high energy and capital costs for processing materials, and high environmental costs in materials production and disposal. Countries that have failed to make progress have generally masked necessity with price controls and trade barriers. Those that have succeeded, however, have turned their handicaps to advantage. They have cut both environmental and economic costs of materials use.

Metals recovery reduces pollution. Using coke in iron ore reduction produces copious quantities of airborne particulates, including carcinogenic substances such as benzopyrene.[10] Recycling iron and steel reduces these particulate emissions by 11 kilograms per metric ton of steel produced. Recycling iron and steel cuts coal and iron ore mining wastes by 11,000 kilograms per metric ton recycled. These solid wastes, unless handled properly, can contaminate surface and groundwaters with acid and toxic metal drainage. Recycling aluminum reduces air emissions associated with aluminum production

"Countries that have failed to make progress in recycling have generally masked necessity with price controls and trade barriers."

by 96 percent. (See Table 1.) By doubling worldwide aluminum recovery rates, over a million tons of air pollutants—including toxic fluoride—would be eliminated.[11]

Table 1: U.S. Environmental Benefits of Recycling[1]

	Paper	Aluminum	Iron & Steel
		(percent)	
Energy Use Reduction	30-55[2]	90-95	60-70
Spoil & Solid Waste Reduction	130[3]	100	95
Air Pollution Reduction	95	95	30

[1]Percent reduction in BTUs, tons of waste, tons of particulates, etc., per ton of material produced from waste. [2]Refers to combustion of both commercial energy and wood residues. [3]More than a 100 percent reduction is possible because 1.3 pounds of waste paper is required to produce one pound of recycled paper. If all paper were recycled, the waste reduction, of course, would equal only 100 percent.

Sources: R.C. Zieglev et al., *Impacts of Virgin and Recycled Steel and Aluminum* (Washington, D.C.: U.S. Environmental Protection Agency, 1976); and *Waste Paper Recovery* (Paris: Organisation for Economic Co-operation and Development, 1979).

Paper recycling helps preserve forests. Paper products use about 35 percent of the world's annual commercial wood harvest, a share that will probably grow to 50 percent by the year 2000.[12] Although a sanguine attitude regarding the state of the world's forests holds a certain following, there is little reason for complacency. The world's tropical hardwood forests will probably decline by 10 percent by the end of the century. The softwood forests of western Russia have long been harvested at nonsustainable rates. The softwood forests of central Europe may be killed by air pollution by 1990, and the resulting decline in wood production will only shift additional pressure to other forests.[13] The United States produces a third of the world's commercial forest products, and its forests would be expected to take up much of this slack. But the harvest of mature softwood forests in the United States has exceeded replacement for several decades. Industry-owned forests, in fact, have been cut so heavily that mature trees have been depleted at an annual rate of 1 to 2 percent, apparently since the early fifties.[14]

Statistics exaggerate the volume and integrity of U.S. forests. In the United States, a forest is defined as an area as small as one acre that is 20 percent covered by trees. Mature softwood trees are defined as trees over nine inches in diameter, though this criterion describes a very young forest. The forests thus may not be as ample as many imagine and may require additional protection. Intensively managed forests will not retain the species diversity of natural forests and will not be as resilient against disease and pollution. Advocates of more intensive harvesting in the United States point out that "growing stock" has been cut at rates far below replacement, but these advocates ignore the fact that, as the *Wall Street Journal* put it, "these forests are neither deep, nor dark, nor lovely."[15] Much of what is called forest can neither satisfy human aesthetic needs nor produce commercial timber.

Paper recycling can help satisfy additional paper needs for years to come. Only 25 percent of the world's paper is now recycled, though no technical or economic reasons prevent the doubling of this share by the end of the century. Recycling half of world paper used today would meet almost 75 percent of new paper demand, and this would free eight million hectares (20 million acres) of forestland from paper production, an area equal to about 5 percent of Europe's forestland. But projections of the future use of the waste paper resource are far less optimistic. Franklin Associates, a consulting firm specializing in paper recycling, projects that recycled paper will supply only 28 percent of world paper production in the year 2000.[16]

Less well known are the economic benefits of materials recycling. Producing paper, aluminum, and iron and steel from secondary in-

"Investing in paper production from waste paper instead of pulp can save about 50 percent of investment costs."

stead of virgin materials typically cuts investment costs by one-half compared to conventional production, and, depending on the product and the country, can cut total costs significantly. Debt-ridden developing countries and their lenders could often double the productivity of the scarce capital available to them by investing in secondary rather than primary materials production. Investing in paper production from waste paper instead of pulp can save about 50 percent of investment costs.[17] Because energy costs also are lower for paper recycling, recycled paper can compete favorably in many paper markets, depending on the cost of collected paper. The initial investment costs for producing aluminum and iron and steel from scrap instead of ore are 25 to 50 percent lower, and total production costs can be 10 to 30 percent lower.

Many nations continue to mask the growing necessity of capturing recycling's benefits. They subsidize energy use with price controls, production tax incentives, and the uncontrolled environmental cost of producing and using energy in materials processing. The full cost of energy-intensive materials is not accurately represented in their prices, and the incentive to reduce these costs is diminished. The true cost of energy includes the cost of damage to forests from acid rain, human health from particulates, human and aquatic populations displaced by hydroelectric projects, and so on. Solid waste disposal costs usually are paid in general taxes, not by persons who create waste, leaving no incentive to reduce the cost of waste. Export barriers have been erected specifically to reduce the price of metal scrap, a measure that reduces the incentive to collect scrap and makes it less available as a substitute for primary materials. Countries performing best in recycling have avoided these pitfalls.

Waste Paper Recycling

World waste paper consumption has increased 140 percent since 1965. Paper consumption has doubled over the same period, however, so the share of paper recycled has changed only slightly, from 20 percent in 1965 to 24 percent in 1982. Despite the world's poor paper recycling record, certain countries have achieved much higher rates of recycling than others. (See Table 2.) Moreover, much progress has been made only in the last ten years. (See Table 3.)

Japan, the Netherlands, Mexico, South Korea, and Portugal lead in waste paper recovery or use. Japan in 1980 collected almost half of the paper it consumed. The Netherlands recovered 44 percent of its paper in 1980, and has led the world for decades in paper recycling.[18]

Why do some countries perform better than others? "Fiber rich" countries such as Canada, Norway, the United States, and Sweden have not excelled, recycling 18, 23, 26, and 34 percent, respectively. The United States, however, is in a category by itself. Though it recycles only a quarter of its paper, it nevertheless leads the world in exporting waste paper.

The admirable paper recycling performance of Japan, South Korea, Mexico, the Netherlands, and Portugal has been predictably promoted by necessity. These "fiber poor" countries, without substantial forests available for pulp wood harvesting, have been pressed by price and scarcity to conserve waste paper. This may be partly a matter of choice for the Japanese since they have substantial forests on their northern islands that they do not heavily exploit. South Korea has made great strides in reforestation, but still places heavy demand on its forests, especially for firewood.[19] South Korea, Portugal, and Mexico doubly contribute to waste paper recovery: They have high national rates of waste paper recovery, and they import waste paper.

"Markets first, collections second," should be the philosophy of recyclers, according to Ronald Rosenson of the National Association of Recycling Industries in the United States.[20] That is, the first priority in materials recycling policy should be to establish demand for recyclable products. If markets are established, collection will follow.

Countries successful in recycling, however, have simultaneously established markets and encouraged collection with strong measures.

Table 2: Paper Use and Waste Paper Recycling, Selected Countries, 1978-80

	Annual Paper Consumption Per Capita	Recovery Rate*
	(pounds)	(percent)
Mexico	n.a.	50
Japan	326	45
Netherlands	347	43
Spain	156	40
South Korea	87	38
Hungary	132	37
West Germany	346	35
Sweden	477	34
Italy	205	29
Brazil	64	29
Australia	295	28
United States	580	26
Canada	417	18
Philippines	22	16
Nigeria	7	2
World Estimate	80	24

*Waste paper collected as a percent of paper consumption, three-year average, 1978-80.

Source: *Waste Paper Data, 1978-80* (Rome: Food and Agriculture Organization of the United Nations, April 1981).

Table 3: Waste Paper Recovery in Selected Countries, 1960-80[1]

	1960	1965	1970	1974[2]	1980[3]
Australia	n.a.	16	n.a.	23	28
Austria	22	25	30	30	33
Canada	16	15	19	18	19
Denmark	21	13	18	28	27
France	27	27	28	31	30
West Germany	27	27	30	32	35
Italy	15	17	21	28	30
Japan	n.a.	37	39	39	47
Netherlands	34	34	40	46	44
Norway	16	20	17	21	22
Spain	25	28	28	32	38
Sweden	26	21	22	28	33
Switzerland	33	33	31	40	35
United Kingdom	28	29	29	28	34
United States	n.a.	22	21	24[2]	27
World Estimate	n.a.	20	21	24	25

[1]Waste paper collected as a percent of paper consumption. [2]Data for 1975 unavailable, except for United States. [3]These values are for 1980 only; Table 2 provides an average value for 1978 through 1980.

Sources: Organisation for Economic Co-operation and Development [1960-1974]; United Nations Food and Agriculture Organization [1980].

Success in Japan and the Netherlands has been motivated by twin necessities. In addition to being "fiber poor," both are crowded, land-poor countries with populations strongly opposed to waste dumps. These factors together drove up both the economic and the political costs of wasting paper. Importing finished paper was expensive, and the Japanese people passionately opposed location of dumps near their homes, making it politically costly for leaders to override residents' protests. The Dutch have similarly opposed landfill disposal of municipal waste. Since 20 to 40 percent of Japanese and Dutch municipal solid waste is paper, paper recycling offers a considerable reduction in waste disposal problems.

Japan's success in recycling began with the pressure of demand, since Japan is the world's second largest consumer of paper. But citizen pressure for environmental protection played a key role. Demand for waste reduction and forest protection pushed Japan into recycling as much as markets pulled it to a high rate of paper recovery. The market for waste paper created by the high paper demand and scarce forest resources satisfied the first criterion. The solution of the second criterion, effective collection, has been achieved with surprising diversity. This suggests that collection can be made to work in any number of circumstances, as long as collected waste can be sold for a reasonable price.

Japan's efforts in recycling have historical roots but began in earnest in the mid-sixties. Now about 10 percent of Japan's total municipal waste is recycled, and efforts are continuing to increase this proportion. One of the first programs in Japan resulted from the efforts of a private entrepreneur who in 1966 persuaded the government of Ueda City to pay him a portion of the "avoided costs" of landfilling the materials that his firm recycled. The avoided cost is the expense saved by waste reduction. The city found it cheaper to pay a small recycling incentive than to pay a larger amount for waste disposal. The plan requires residents to separate refuse into combustible and noncombustible material. Glass is separated by hand at the dump and ferrous metal removed by magnet. Overall, refuse disposal has dropped by 8 percent.[21]

Hiroshima has achieved stunning success: disposal of raw refuse has been reduced by 40 percent since 1976. The City Environmental Project Bureau helped organize participation of student clubs, parent-teacher organizations, and similar groups to teach and encourage citizens to sort and prepare their garbage for collection. These organizations contract with waste haulers who deliver the material to recyclers or to the city. Payments go to the nonprofit groups at or above market rates, with a subsidy made possible by savings from avoided landfill fees. Citizens are urged to sort their trash into three main categories: paper, nonreturnable bottles and cans, and noncombustibles. Paper is carried to local paper collection centers located within a few blocks of most residents throughout the city. Other items are placed in special bins and are collected separately.[22]

The size and density of Hiroshima's population (878,000) obviously has facilitated its recycling success. The small, less densely populated suburban town of Mizuho, however, with a population of only 22,000, reported similar results. As in Hiroshima, citizens' organizations are used to encourage recycling. But instead of paying groups for garbage recycled, the city itself contracts for collection. Recyclables are then sold, with the city keeping 40 percent of the revenues and paying 60 percent to the community groups responsible for promoting source separation.[23]

Another means of overcoming obstacles to collection has been demonstrated in Fuchu city, a suburb of Tokyo with a population of 187,000. The city purchased the necessary recycling equipment and pays a company a fixed fee for its operation. Thus, the obstacle of an insurmountably large up-front capital requirement for the private firm was avoided. An incentive to increase the firm's performance was added by allowing the firm to keep 20 percent of the revenues earned from the sale of recycled materials above the cost of collecting the refuse and operating the facility. In the Shiki district, the government also made the initial capital investment in equipment, but turned its operation over to a firm to which it pays no fee. Instead, the firm earns all of its revenues from sales of recyclables.

"The Japanese make it easy to participate and difficult not to participate in paper recycling."

"We have to change [wasteful] culture from the very roots," asserts Muneo Matsumoto, an official in Machida, "the garbage capital of Japan." Machida boasts that its new recycling program of source separation and computerized processing recycles 90 percent of the city's garbage.[24] Progress such as this flows from the legendary discipline of the Japanese, their proclivity for efficiency, and their willingness to cooperate and solve problems. The grassroots information system provided by citizens and citizens' groups works well, apparently as a result of the incentives provided the groups. The Japanese make it easy to participate and difficult not to participate in paper recycling.

The Netherlands' approach to waste paper collection has been different from Japan's, but has been just as successful. As in Japan, necessity motivated national and local governments to ensure waste paper recycling: Both fiber resources and land for waste disposal have been scarce. The Netherlands has historically achieved the best paper recycling record in the world, using a few key policies to make the marketplace work better. For example, the government established the world's first waste exchange, a free brokerage service to match buyers and sellers of waste. The government has also attempted to stabilize the typical boom and bust cycles in recyclables by establishing "buffer stocks." The recycling industry is particularly vulnerable to wild cyclical swings in the market, and the recent recession has been the worst for the recycling industry since the Great Depression. Buffer stocks enable collectors of waste paper to sell to the government-established fund when prices drop below a predetermined level. The stock is sold when prices go up again, and the fund is thereby replenished.[25] Some economists say this approach is costly and sometimes counterproductive. It is difficult to match its operation with the needs of the market and thus to avoid undesired market distortions. Yet, the approach has been used both in Japan and the Netherlands, the two leading nations in paper recycling, and may merit further consideration.[26]

The Netherlands strongly promotes source separation, though differently from Japan. Whereas Japan has relied more on awareness, information, incentives, and armies of nonprofit organizations, the Netherlands simply enacted a law requiring source separation in all municipalities that have contracted for collection of waste paper. This fact reinforces the observation that any number of policies may be applied to effect recycling once societies decide to do it.

Mandatory source separation has recently been applied with success in the United States. Islip, New York, was sued by the state to halt landfilling, partly because its landfill was contaminating underground water and releasing vinyl chloride into the air.[27] A court settlement required the city to initiate recycling. In a program dubbed WRAP, for Wednesday Recyclables Are Picked (Up), residents may be fined up to $250 for noncompliance.[28] No major enforcement actions have yet been needed, however, because a 50 percent compliance rate has exceeded the city's capability to handle recyclables. Five inspectors patrol the collection and issue warning tickets to households failing to comply. A household that has been warned several times but does not cooperate eventually will face noncollection of its garbage.[29] The collection program, moreover, has succeeded without costly investments in sophisticated engineering devices. Residents simply place recyclables in containers with glass and cans on top and paper underneath. The city sorts ferrous material with magnets and the rest by hand, as in Ueda City, Japan.

To encourage market development, the Scandinavian countries have a cooperative waste exchange; Sweden, in fact, helps industries with hazardous wastes find buyers who can put the material to productive use.[30] A West German waste exchange founded in 1974 has brokered over 20,000 offers and requests for recyclable materials, and has expanded into Austria, Switzerland, northern Italy, and France.[31] But the experience in most of these countries suggests that information and market assistance, though necessary, are not sufficient to reach high levels of materials recycling.

Necessity is the mother of collection, and uneven distribution of the world's forest resources provides some nations with local abundance

"In South Korea, imported waste paper provides 40 percent of the fiber used in paper production."

despite global scarcity. But just as wasting gasoline in an oil rich country carries an opportunity cost in lost export sales, so does waste of recyclable paper. If properly promoted, the new international market for waste paper could supply a strong incentive to collect waste paper in all countries. The recent growth of international trade marks an important step in waste paper market development. International waste paper trade has grown from almost nothing in the early seventies to about 10 percent of all waste paper collected, or 2 to 3 percent of all paper used in the world. The value of this trade totals some $600 million, depending upon volatile market prices.[32]

South Korea and Mexico now produce half of their paper from waste paper, and in South Korea, imported waste paper provides 40 percent of the fiber used in paper production. Almost half of Italy's paper production depends on waste paper, a significant portion of which is imported. Canada imports half of the waste paper it uses. This, unfortunately, is a consequence of the low collection rate within its own borders. Unlike Canada, most countries that import waste paper have high internal rates of waste paper collection. (See Table 2.) Collection rates in Japan, the Netherlands, South Korea, and Mexico are the highest in the world. The high percentages achieved in these countries are all the more remarkable considering that much of the paper they consume is exported as packaging for manufactured goods.

The United States now dominates the international waste paper trade, accounting for 85 percent of net sales. The significant expansion of trade between the United States, Mexico, South Korea, and Japan during the seventies can serve as a model for development of waste paper trade elsewhere.

China, for example, might offer an enormous market for waste paper exporters. Demand for paper will increase as China develops, but forest resources to meet this demand with virgin pulp will be lacking. Similarly, India, the Philippines, and Thailand could become large markets for recyclable paper.[33] But obstacles to trade could effectively block this development. Though trade in waste paper has so far met with few serious constraints, several factors have kept it below its potential. South Korea, for example, imposes a 10 percent import fee on waste paper. Because this paper comes largely from the United States and shipping rates are extremely favorable on this route, the tariff has not caused paper exporters great difficulties. Under less favorable transportation terms, however, tariffs and constraints on licensing imports would hinder recycling. Transportation, in fact, has been the greatest impediment so far. Waste paper trade between the United States and Venezuela has been crippled by high rates, and inadequate rail and road facilities have hampered trade between the United States and Mexico. Another significant impediment has been unstable currency exchange rates. High values for the U.S. dollar have reduced U.S. exports of waste paper.[34]

Paper recycling can be promoted by creating or widening cost advantages for recycled paper over paper made from virgin pulp. One advantage could be provided by increasing the price of virgin wood pulp to reflect its true economic value. In nations where mature softwood forests are harvested faster than replacement, reducing the rate of harvest would raise the price of pulp closer to its long-term economic value. Forests would thus be afforded greater protection and waste paper recycling would be encouraged. Paper and wood prices need not increase as long as additional quantities of waste paper are recovered and recycled.

The United States government could make a major contribution to this policy, since it owns half of all U.S. softwood forests. The U.S. Forest Service significantly affects the price of pulp by leasing large areas of national forests each year regardless of market demand. The suspension or modification of this practice, coupled with setting aside more publicly-owned forests for wilderness and parkland, would reduce the environmental subsidy of the use of virgin pulp and increase the relative attractiveness of waste paper. The United States may also find it particularly advantageous to acquire and protect forests in the Southeast where wood harvesting is growing rapidly.

"Nations with waste paper to sell must assure would-be buyers that waste paper exports will not be restricted by protectionism."

The price of waste paper can be stablized by increasing demand for it and by expanding its collection. Higher, more stable prices would provide an incentive for commercial waste paper collection. Local zoning ordinances to reduce landfill disposal of paper wastes, coupled with broader regional or national laws requiring source separation and mandatory collection of waste paper, will increase waste paper supplies and thus serve to prevent drastic price increases. Indeed, the greater problem will be to maintain demand for waste paper. International markets will be essential for this purpose. On the other hand, there is a risk that widespread use of waste paper as a fuel in resource recovery plants could push its price to levels that would preclude its use in paper production.

Waste paper will not be used unless there is the means to use it, and this implies that a marked change is needed in investment strategies in the papermaking process. Following World War II, most Canadian and U.S. paper makers built mills to exploit virgin pulp. A different type of mill is required to make paper from waste. Private companies will be induced to build recycling mills mainly by policies that increase the price difference between virgin pulp and waste paper.

In developing countries, however, using cheap waste paper, domestic or imported, rather than imported pulp or finished paper products, has already proven economically attractive. International development agencies and financial institutions have begun to recognize the cost-cutting potential of investment in waste paper recycling in the Third World. The World Bank in 1982 contributed almost $1 million to improve the efficiency with which Egypt's outcasts and garbage pickers, the Zebaleen, collect Cairo's wastes. The World Bank has also supported a multi-million dollar project in Egypt that will recycle paper.[35] Investments in recycling waste paper in developing countries will lead to higher rates of international waste paper collection by creating a ready market. Nations with waste paper to sell must assure would-be buyers that waste paper exports will not be restricted by protectionism.

Government procurement of recycled paper stimulates recycling. Existing law requires the U.S. government to purchase paper made from recycled fibers, but the Carter and Reagan administrations have ignored this requirement. The state government of Maryland, however, has effectively complied with a similar law. Twenty-five percent of the state's paper now is recycled paper. The Organisation for Economic Co-operation and Development also encourages procurement of recycled paper for its own and its 24 member nations' uses.[36]

The use of waste paper as a fuel has created a unique problem, what J. Rodney Edwards of the American Paper Institute calls "the worst threat to paper recycling." This threat is "flow control" or government monopoly of the flow of waste materials. The opposition to and cost of landfilling has drawn municipal governments to the use of resource recovery systems, which burn refuse to produce energy. But some cities have gone beyond using refuse, and would burn paper now being recycled. Akron, Ohio, for example, has built a resource recovery plant and has fought to control all waste products in the city. The plant's creditors successfully pressured the city to ensure that all burnable waste would flow to the facility in order to increase the revenues generated by its energy sales. This meant that recyclers collecting old newspapers, cuttings from envelope manufacturers, or corrugated containers from supermarkets could be forced to deliver recyclable materials to the city dump so that these could be burned instead of recycled. As a fuel, waste paper has a value of about $20 per ton, while recyclable paper has a value of $40 to $60 per ton or more.

The Japanese, the Dutch, and others widely use incineration and energy recovery, but only after collection of recyclable waste paper. These facilities can be sized in advance to account for paper removed for recycling. If they are not, however, cities will have a powerful incentive to discourage recycling. Many U.S. facilities were planned in the energy crisis atmosphere of the seventies. But, as David Brower, founder of Friends of the Earth, said as he spoke in opposition to a resource recovery plant in his home town, they may be "a

"When governments attempt to control energy prices, not only is energy wasted, but recyling becomes less attractive."

good idea whose time has passed."[37] Some U.S. advocates of recycling call for a federal law to protect recyclers from monopoly control of municipalities' wastes. Since the United States has 34 energy recovery facilities in operation, 20 nearing completion, and many others under consideration in communities facing shortages of landfill space, millions of tons of recyclable waste paper could soon be "wasted" in municipal incinerators.

When governments attempt to control energy prices, not only is energy wasted, but recycling becomes less attractive. The United States, for example, controls the price of natural gas, which ranks second only to waste wood as a fuel for the U.S. paper industry. As a result, the industry uses more natural gas and less waste wood to produce paper. Paper prices do not reflect the true energy costs of production, and this in turn lowers the rate of paper recycling by decreasing the relative value of waste paper. Because the U.S. produces one-third of the world's paper, U.S. natural gas price policy reduces waste paper demand throughout the world.[38]

Market development will remain a top priority for promoting waste paper recycling. Capital investment, advertising, procurement practices, free trade, promotion, and pricing policies will all be required. But policies do not "just happen." Policy implementation increasingly requires promotion by both economic interests and citizens' organizations.

Aluminum Recycling

The meaning of the Promethean myth becomes clearer in the making of aluminum, one of the most important metals to mankind. Many aspects of modern civilization, such as air travel, would be virtually impossible without affordable aluminum. Substituting aluminum for heavy steel in automobiles saves gasoline. Substituting aluminum for glass or steel packaging saves energy in transportation and may allow easier, more efficient recycling. Yet aluminum produced from bauxite requires 20 times as much electricity as aluminum produced from recycled metal. Bauxite and coal must be strip mined in the process, and rivers are often dammed to generate hydroelectric power for smelting. Discarded aluminum containers spoil the environment. Despite these problems, aluminum will play an important role in any industrial society, and so its efficient production and use are essential.

The world is far from achieving the technical potential for aluminum recycling. Some analysts estimate that 80 percent of all aluminum used can be recycled. But less than 30 percent of world production came from recycled scrap in 1981. Even so, half of all aluminum recycled came from industrial wastes—scrap produced in the smelting or cutting and fabrication of finished products.

The low worldwide rate of aluminum recycling is caused in part by rapid growth in the production of durable consumer items such as appliances. These products last many years and so do not soon yield their metal to recycling. Purchases of washing machines, refrigerators, and automobiles in Brazil in the early seventies grew at an annual rate of 24 percent.[39] Countries such as Brazil, moving from low to high per capita rates of aluminum consumption, or experiencing high rates of population growth, can expect somewhat lower rates of aluminum available for recovery. But many countries such as Norway, Australia, and Canada have had high per capita rates of aluminum consumption for years, yet recycle relatively small amounts. (See Table 4.) Low recycling rates in these countries may be due to historically low energy prices.

Since energy accounts for 20 percent of the cost of producing aluminum from virgin ore, the progress made in recycling in the seventies can be explained in part by energy price increases. (See Figure 1.) Great strides have been made in the United States, illustrating that modern society can adapt to increasing scarcity without sacrificing living standards. U.S. aluminum recycling has reduced both envi-

"Aluminum produced from bauxite requires 20 times as much electricity as aluminum produced from recycled metal."

ronmental pollution and the need to construct new power facilities, thus freeing scarce capital for use elsewhere in the economy.

Table 4: Aluminum Use and Recycling in Selected Countries, 1981

	Aluminum Consumption Per Capita	Recovery Rate*
	(pounds)	(percent)
The Netherlands	21	42
Italy	27	41
West Germany	45	33
United States	56	32
United Kingdom	20	28
France	26	27
Japan	42	25
Switzerland	34	21
Norway	42	20
Sweden	34	19
Australia	41	16
Canada	36	16
Austria	27	15
Brazil	5	13
Mexico	7	10
World Estimate	7	28

*Aluminum collected as a percent of consumption.

Source: *Aluminum Statistical Review for 1981* (Washington, D.C.: The Aluminum Association, Inc., 1982), pp. 42-62.

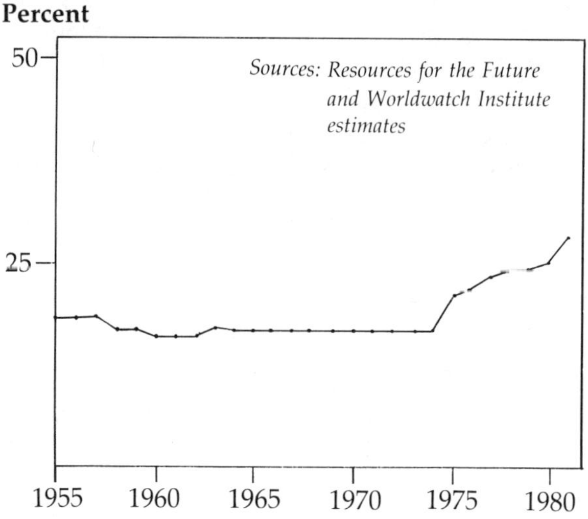

Figure 1: World Aluminum Recycling Rate, 1955-81

The United States, the Soviet Union, Canada, Japan, and West Germany produce 60 percent of the world's aluminum. Adding Norway, France, Spain, Australia, China, Italy, and Great Britain brings this total to over 75 percent.[40] Italy, West Germany, and the United States exhibit the highest rates of secondary aluminum production. Italy produces 50 percent of its aluminum from scrap, while West Germany and the United States produce one-third from recycled aluminum. Italy's performance is particularly impressive because its per capita consumption has long averaged less than half that in the United States and 60 percent that in West Germany.[41]

Norway, often cited as an example of environmental sensitivity, directly recycles only 4 percent of the aluminum it consumes, but ex-

"The United States threw away more recyclable aluminum in the form of beverage cans than all of Africa produced.

ports large quantities of scrap, which brings the total to 20 percent. Much of Norway's scrap aluminum finds its way either directly or indirectly to Italy, indicating the importance of international trade in recyclables. The Soviet Union, the world's second largest aluminum producer, altogether recycled and exported only 10 percent as much aluminum as it consumed in 1979 or 1980. Australia did only slightly better.

These aluminum recovery rates can only provide a relative index of how well a nation has performed. The figures include scrap from fabricating mills, so-called "prompt scrap," and this undoubtedly overstates progress in each major producing country. Nevertheless, the dramatic differences between countries, especially those with high rates of production and consumption, can be instructive.

The pattern of recycling clearly corresponds with energy prices. The United States only ten years ago ranked low among the world's major aluminum producers. (See Table 5.) Subsidized hydroelectric power, cheap coal, and the advent of nuclear power plants kept electricity prices low. But coal price increases and nuclear power plant cost overruns in the aluminum producing Tennessee Valley and Pacific Northwest greatly increased the cost of power and thus made the production of primary aluminum more costly.[42] These power cost increases had a dramatic effect on aluminum recycling: recycling grew from 17 percent to 32 percent in ten years. The rate of growth in secondary aluminum production averaged 6.4 percent each year in the last decade compared to 2.3 percent for aluminum.[43] U.S. scrap consumption jumped a prodigous 17.7 percent in 1981. The most dramatic change came in recycled aluminum cans: only 15 percent of all aluminum cans were recycled in the United States in 1972, but over half were recycled in 1981.[44] The United States recycled as much aluminum can scrap in 1981 as the entire continent of Africa produced in both primary and secondary smelters. This also means, of course, that the United States threw away more recyclable aluminum in the form of beverage cans than all of Africa produced.[45]

Table 5: Aluminum Recycling in Selected Countries, 1954-81[1]

	1954	1960	1965	1970	1975	1981
			(percent)			
France	21	19	17	20	23	27
West Germany	45	39	39	34	30	33
Italy	27	29	33	37	41	41
Japan	19	26	29	28	n.a.	25
United Kingdom	30	32	36	35	30	28
United States	18	16	17	17	26	32
World Estimate	19	16	17	17	21	28

[1]These countries represent 50 percent of world aluminum production. Recycling rates represent secondary recovery, including scrap aluminum consumed in both primary and secondary production, and net scrap exports, as a percent of aluminum consumption.

Sources: Leonard L. Fischman, *World Mineral Trends and U.S. Supply Problems* (Washington, D.C.: Resources for the Future, 1980) [through 1970]; and *Aluminum Statistical Review for 1981* (Washington, D.C.: The Aluminum Association, Inc., 1982). [1975-1981].

Norway is the world's sixth largest aluminum producer and is fourth highest in per capita aluminum consumption. Yet it recovers only 20 percent of the aluminum it consumes. This poor record is probably due to Norway's abundance of inexpensive hydroelectric power. Though the long-term migration of energy intensive industries to energy rich countries such as Norway may be a positive step toward a sustainable society, in the current era of unattained recycling potential, it presents a hidden pitfall.[46] Whether subsidies for energy use come in the form of energy price regulations, government and development bank financing of hydroelectric facilities, or environmental degradation from flooding, species extinction, and fuel combustion, they unnecessarily waste resources. The low worldwide rate of aluminum recycling suggests that energy projects planned in order to permit additional primary aluminum production are unnecessary. Ten years of environmental opposition to hydroelectric development in Norway has led to reduced expansion of primary aluminum production there.[47] Similarly, opposition halted a dam designed to produce power for aluminum smelting in Tasmania.[48] These actions, ironically, may increase the availability of affordable aluminum since they will force a more economical use of resources.

Despite high energy costs, Japan recycles only about 25 percent of the aluminum it consumes. But per capita aluminum consumption has been low in Japan until the last decade, when rates climbed sharply. Much of Japan's "consumption," in fact, is shipped out of the country in manufactured products such as automobiles. The Japanese mainly use steel cans and glass bottles for beverages, and so less aluminum scrap is available than in the U.S. On the other hand, Japan's primary aluminum industry has seriously lost its ability to compete--as has Italy's. Japan generates electricity with oil, so power there now costs more than in most countries. Japanese primary aluminum production, as a result, has dropped by about 25 percent over the last ten years, and the industry's losses in 1982 totalled over $500 million.[49] Less than 20 percent of the industry's primary aluminum production capacity, in fact, is deemed competitive.[50] In 1981, the Japanese actually produced more aluminum from secondary metal than from primary sources. One-quarter of the scrap processed was imported from the United States: bringing back parts of the Toyotas and Datsuns, as it were. In the meantime, Japan has imposed tariffs on imported aluminum ingot, and has pursued investment in primary aluminum production in seven countries. Japan's share in these investments assures Japanese companies as much primary aluminum production as Japan used in 1982 (872,000 tons per year).[51] Italy's primary aluminum industry has tottered on the brink of collapse for several years, and the secondary industry may be the only remaining healthy segment.[52]

Low levels of aluminum recycling in the Soviet Union may be attributed to the complicated and highly centralized control of materials production and allocation, and to energy price distortions similar to those caused by energy price controls in effect in the United States during the seventies.[53]

As with waste paper, international trade brings a new and dynamic force to the recovery of scrap aluminum. Scrap moving across national boundaries in 1980 totalled 820,000 tons, representing more than 5 percent of world aluminum production.[54] With the price of scrap at 36¢ per pound, the value of internationally traded aluminum scrap amounted to almost $600 million in 1980.[55]

Three leading consumers of recycled aluminum—Japan, West Germany, and Italy—all import large quantities of aluminum scrap. The volume of scrap imported by Japan in 1981 equalled Japan's volume of aluminum consumption ten years earlier. With primary production declining as a result of oil price increases, secondary production in Japan has increased 138 percent over the last decade, with as much as 70 percent of this increase made possible by scrap imports. Twenty percent of both West Germany's and Italy's total aluminum production in 1980 can be attributed to aluminum scrap imports. European scrap smelters, nevertheless, pose a threat to the free trade of aluminum. Seeking lower scrap prices, they argue for increased trade barriers to restrict exports from their countries. A trade publication of the secondary smelter industry reports that "EEC secondary smelters are . . . endeavouring to ensure that the export of high value and energy-rich raw material is restricted by the re-introduction of export quotas." These quotas were removed by EEC countries in 1981 and replaced with a less restrictive export licensing system. Exports of aluminum doubled after these trade restrictions were eased.[56]

The importance of trade to the growth of recycling is clear. If the strategy for recyclers is "markets first, collection second," then that strategy will be defeated by efforts to suppress aluminum scrap prices. Such an approach has historically plagued the iron and steel scrap industry. The importance of recycling aluminum cans also is clear. Fully a quarter of all U.S. aluminum production goes into

"Deposits are now required on all beverage containers sold in Sweden, Denmark, Norway, the Netherlands and several provinces in Canada."

packaging, half of this into beverage containers. Whereas Mexicans in 1981 used about 6.5 pounds of aluminum per capita for all uses, Americans used 6.7 pounds per capita for beverage containers alone.[57] And while packaging can be an important means of protecting food and other products, unless recycled, such consumption would not seem to be sustainable.

The private sector has made commendable progress in collecting aluminum cans for recycling. One of the most exciting innovations in recycling is the "reverse vending machine." The machine accepts aluminum cans, rejects ferrous cans, glass, or other unwanted objects, weighs the aluminum deposited and dispenses money or coupons in payment. One machine in Dickenson, South Dakota, reclaimed 109 tons of cans in one year, and 20 reverse vending machines in Denver, Colorado, paid out over $1 million in an 18-month period.[58] Sweden reportedly will build and install an estimated 10,000 reverse vending machines as part of an effort to recover 75 percent of all aluminum cans used in the country. This would save 10,000 tons of aluminum annually (500 million cans), equal to Sweden's annual aluminum imports.[59]

The Colorado-based Coors Brewery makes a special effort to recycle cans: It has a contract with its aluminum supplier that provides a discount in return for recovered aluminum. Coors opened eight recycling centers in Atlanta, Georgia, even before it sold products there. In fact, the company each year collects more than 50,000 tons of aluminum cans in more than 20 states.[60]

Though it is encouraging that Americans now recycle 54 percent of the cans they use, countries and individual states with container deposit legislation have made much more dramatic gains. Deposits are now required on all beverage containers sold in Sweden, Denmark, Norway, the Netherlands, and several provinces in Canada. Nine states in the United States now require deposits on beverage containers, and the recent addition of New York, the second most populous state, to this list represents major progress for recycling. (See Table 6.) Return rates of both bottles and cans exceed 90 percent in most states, almost twice the U.S. national rate.[61]

In almost all states with container deposit laws, total litter has been reduced by 35 to 40 percent by volume, and beverage container litter by 75 to 86 percent by number of pieces. In Oregon, the U.S. pioneer in this policy, a net total of 200 jobs were created. In Michigan, the first state to test container legislation in a densely populated urban setting, 4,600 jobs were created. No state with a bottle bill has lost jobs on a net basis. A nationwide beverage container law in the United States would, according to the U.S. General Accounting Office, create a net total of 100,000 jobs. As an additional benefit, litter cleanup costs in Maine were reduced by 50 percent. For all these reasons, almost three-quarters of the U.S. population favors enactment of container legislation.[62]

Promoting the use of aluminum containers in preference to others might actually conserve resources. The steel can, when it is tin plated, is so difficult to recycle that even the recycling industry calls it "a can of worms."[63] "Tin" cans, which are mostly steel with a thin coating of tin to prevent corrosion, are not easily recyclable because the tin fuses with the steel. Most recycled tin cans, in fact, are used as a catalyst in copper production. The metal in the cans is actually consumed in the process and cannot be recovered.

The aluminum can, which is readily recyclable, could beneficially replace steel-alloy or bimetal cans, and even glass. Though reusing bottles saves large amounts of energy, recycling glass saves only small amounts of energy. Unless a returnable bottle is re-used ten times, it offers no energy savings over recycled aluminum cans. Aluminum, because it is more amenable to recycling, could replace the steel and glass now used for food containers and would thus save energy and materials. Ways would have to be devised to strengthen aluminum cans to prevent denting or collapse. Aluminum beverage cans retain their shape in part due to the pressure provided by car-

Table 6: U.S. States with Beverage Container Deposit Laws and Their Container Return Rates

	Effective Date	Refillable Bottles	Cans
		(percent)	
Oregon	1972	95	92
Vermont	1973	93	90
Maine	1978	93	93
Michigan	1979	96	96
Iowa	1979	96	90
Connecticut	1980	—	—
Massachusetts	1983	—	—
Delaware	1983	—	—
New York	1983	—	—

Sources: William K. Shireman, *Can and Bottle Bills* (Stanford, Calif.: California Public Interest Research Group and Stanford Environmental Law Society, 1981), p. 193; and "State Experience With Beverage Container Deposit Laws Show Positive Benefits," U.S. Congress, General Accounting Office (PAD-81-08), December 11, 1980, pp. 16, 40.

bonated gas in the beverages, and some analysts believe that liquid nitrogen placed in cans containing noncarbonated products could serve the same purpose.[64] The energy required to produce aluminum cans is comparable with refillable glass bottles on an ounce-for-ounce basis, and is lower than for steel cans.[65] Thus, the ongoing switch to aluminum cans for beverage containers might bring resource conservation benefits as might a similar switch in food containers.

Several exotic metals are used as aluminum alloys. Magnesium and manganese add strength and workability to aluminum, making it satisfactory for can production. Copper and zinc add high strength and corrosion resistance, making aluminum ideal for use in airplanes, spaceships, and automobiles. A combination of magnesium and silicon makes aluminum a useful substitute for copper electrical cable. The production of these alloys presents an opportunity to recover these exotic metals in aluminum recycling, but also creates a problem by contaminating aluminum.

Aluminum products each have strict specifications for the amount of other metals that may be present. Aerospace or auto scrap with 1 to 2 percent zinc could not simply be melted and then used to produce beverage containers. Recycling the various alloys requires sophisticated testing, sorting, and blending of scrap to produce acceptable new alloys. Stainless steel, free zinc, and magnesium, all of which may be mixed with scrap in the collection process, contaminate aluminum and thus impede recycling. Magnesium can be refined out of aluminum, but the process produces fluoride air emissions and is expensive. Stainless steel is nonmagnetic and is difficult to detect. The long-term recycling of aluminum and of its alloys will increasingly depend on the development of improved means of sorting and refining scrap.

Growth in recycling will depend on both market development and scrap collection. International markets, especially in developing countries, could provide the impetus for increasing collection in countries with high consumption rates. Investments in secondary recovery can be encouraged by international lending agencies, nations desiring to improve their balance of trade, entrepreneurs, and environmentalists. International banks could exploit this opportunity to promote environmentally acceptable growth with a technology that can produce aluminum for half the capital cost of primary facilities and only 5 percent of the energy operating costs. But the World Bank, for example, has apparently all but ignored this potential in its forthcoming "World Aluminum Industry Study," preferring instead to ask traditional questions about how much new electric capacity investment will be required to run primary facilities.[66]

National governments, moreover, seem interested mainly in primary aluminum production. The response of the Ministry of International

"Use of the electric arc furnace has grown dramatically in those countries with the highest steel recycling rates."

Trade and Industry in Japan to the high cost of primary production in Japan has been to move the industry to developing countries with cheap hydroelectric power.

Secondary aluminum provides an alternative to environmentally troublesome additional primary aluminum production. But taking advantage of the alternative will require investing time and money in campaigns to enact container deposit legislation, assuring free trade in scrap, and devising energy pricing policies that reflect the real economic cost of energy.

Iron and Steel Recycling

Detroit, according to the cartoon strip *Shoe,* is the Saudi Arabia of scrap.[67] This is not just hyperbole, for automobiles junked each year in the United States produce scrap equal to 4 percent of world steel production.

The amount of scrap recycled in the three major steel-making technologies differs dramatically. The open hearth furnace generally uses about 45 percent scrap and 55 percent iron ore. The basic oxygen furnace uses only 28 percent scrap, the rest made up of virgin ore. The electric arc furnace, however, can use virtually 100 percent scrap. Use of the open hearth, the old workhorse of the steel industry, declined dramatically following World War II, giving way to the less scrap-efficient basic oxygen furnace.[68] The basic oxygen furnace produced only 4 percent of U.S. steel in 1960, but now produces over 61 percent, a trend that has diminished recycling. The use of the electric arc furnace also grew over the same period, from 8 to 28 percent of U.S. production, and has had the opposite effect.[69] Use of the electric arc furnace has grown dramatically around the world, especially in those countries with the highest steel recycling rates.

The electric arc furnace offers powerful advantages. Energy costs are cut by 75 percent, capital requirements are cut in half, and finished steel can have a price advantage of as much as a $180 per ton over conventionally produced steels. The electric arc furnace should be attractive in debt-ridden countries needing to invest in steel production.[70]

The world steel industry now uses scrap for 45 percent of its iron requirements, and many countries rate high marks for iron and steel recycling.[71] Those with the best records use scrap for 60 to 75 percent of the metal used in steel making, if steel mill scrap is included. But steel mill scrap basically just recirculates in the production process, meaning that these percentages are cut by half if only purchased scrap—scrap from fabricators and consumers—is counted. Post-consumer scrap recovery represents only one-quarter of all iron and steel recycled, and if the United states is any indication, only 45 percent of the iron and steel that becomes obsolete, or ready for recycling following consumer use, is actually recycled each year.[72] Moreover, this rate is only half as high as in 1955. (See Figure 2.)

One measure of the lack of progress in iron and steel recycling, in fact, is the increase in the stock of obsolete scrap available for but not being used in recycling. In 1978, the backlog of recoverable ferrous scrap in the United States alone totalled over 600 million tons. Since then, this backlog has grown to 680 million tons, and should continue to grow.[73]

Certain countries appear to have far worse recycling records than others in iron and steel. Among Eastern Bloc nations, Czechoslovakia, Poland, East Germany, and Hungary consume scrap at relatively high rates. The Soviet Union, however, ranks as one of the lowest users of scrap in the world with a rate half that of the United States, or the United Kingdom. China, Argentina, Brazil, and Yugoslavia consume very low levels of scrap. Necessity again appears to be at work, for countries with sufficient indigenous sources of iron ore do less recycling. (See Table 7.)

"The electric arc furnace should be attractive in debt-ridden countries needing to invest in steel production."

Table 7: Steel Consumption and Scrap Recycling in Selected Countries, 1980-1982

	Annual Steel Consumption Per Capita	Recovery Rate
	(pounds)	(percent*)
Belgium-Luxembourg	714	40
United Kingdom	715	35
United States	1,120	35
Netherlands	723	35
Japan	1,387	31
Poland	1,162	31
Czechoslovakia	1,607	30
Spain	514	29
West Germany	1,210	27
Italy	1,010	24
Sweden	1,096	24
Brazil	291	21
India	40	18
Soviet Union	1,250	17
China	99	9
World Estimate	400	25

*Represents steel scrap collected (excluding recirculating steel mill scrap and including net exports) as a percent of steel consumed; three-year average.

Sources: Worldwatch estimates from *Minerals Yearbook, 1981, Vol III, Statistical Abstracts, 1983,* and published data provided by the Bureau International de la Recuperation.

But using iron ore because it is available may be a false economy. Scrap costs little more than iron ore and can be converted to steel with

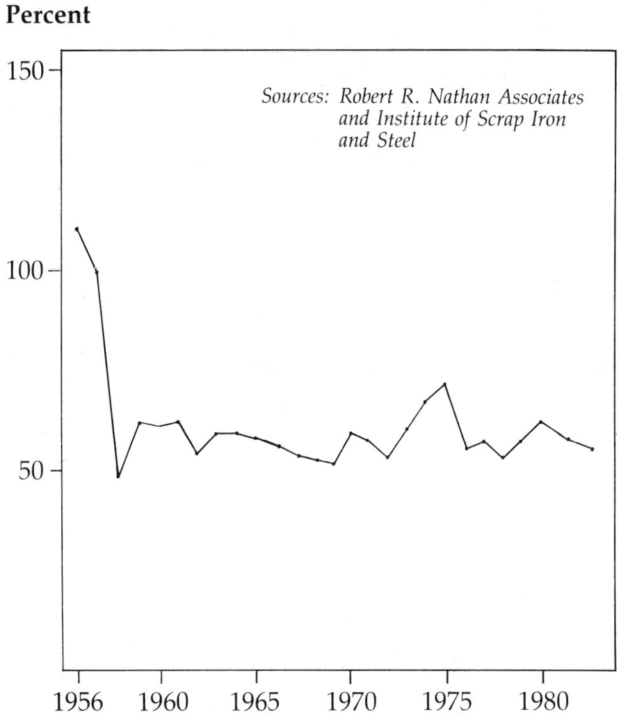

Figure 2: U.S. Iron and Steep Scrap Collected, 1956-1981 (as a percent of scrap generated)

much lower capital costs. The most vibrant sector of the U.S. steel industry, in fact, is the "minimill," which includes electric arc furnaces using scrap. The Nucor mill in North Carolina is a good example, earning a large profit in 1982 during one of the worst years ever in the steel industry.

"Export restrictions threaten the $11 billion world ferrous scrap industry."

A valuable new iron ore reduction technique, direct reduction of iron (DRI), eliminates coking and reduces energy costs. The pig iron produced by DRI is even called artificial scrap. Many countries, including Brazil and Nigeria, have adopted this technology. Total capital costs for direct reduction, however, run as high as for conventional steel production. Despite the advantage of scrap-based production, Brazil still has one of the world's lowest rates of scrap utilization. Nigeria has recently moved to eliminate its dependence on imported steel by investing in direct reduction of iron ore. At a new mill, directly reduced iron is mixed with scrap in four new electric arc furnaces, with scrap supplying 25 percent of the charge. The result has been unsatisfactory, however, since the total cost of Nigerian steel is $880 per ton compared with import prices of $315 to $450. Nigeria might instead have collected more of the large quantities of automobile scrap now rusting in junkyards around the country and processed it in electric arc furnaces. The cost of scrap-based steel would probably have been even lower than the most favorable finished steel import price and only 25 percent of their current production costs.[74] Thus, developing countries with or without iron ore resources should find electric arc production the technology of choice, followed by direct reduction of iron ore.

Developing countries and all nations not well endowed with scrap may perceive that investing in electric arc furnaces is unduly risky. History has shown that scrap exports have been and could easily again be restricted. United States steel makers have consistently sought to keep scrap prices low by lobbying the U.S. government to restrict the export of scrap. Such policies seriously diminish the prospect for iron and steel recycling. They threaten the $11 billion world ferrous scrap industry, in which the United States has the largest stake. In 1980, before the worldwide recession devastated the scrap business, U.S. scrap dealers handled a volume of more than $5 billion worth of scrap, making it the largest recycling market in the world. The United States exports about 15 percent of this total, and this enables the country to dominate world trade in iron and steel scrap. In 1980, the United States exported more than 11 million tons of scrap worth almost $1.3 billion, for 75 percent of the world's net international trade in iron and steel scrap.[75]

U.S. steel makers may have legitimate complaints about unfair trade practices in some steel producing nations. Western Europe, for example, provides extensive subsidies to steel makers, many of which are owned in large part by governments. These subsidies are not reflected in steel prices and therefore not only permit unfair competition but also discourage more cost-effective production, meaning greater use of scrap.[76] Just as the defense of free trade requires maintaining open borders, it requires regulation of unfair trading practices.

Many metals are alloyed with iron to increase its strength, resistance to rusting, and ductility. Stainless steel, which may contain 11.5 to 26 percent chromium, and usually a smaller percent of nickel, is probably the best known alloy. But cobalt and titanium, for example, are increasingly used to add high strength and corrosion resistance in applications such as aerospace that require high performance. Molybdenum and vanadium make alloyed steels useful in structures and machine tools. Sorting, separating, and reprocessing these alloys has become a sophisticated business.

Scrap processors now use shredders, flotation devices, melting furnaces, and other equipment to prepare complex mixtures of scrap metals for recycling. An automobile, for example, contains not only iron and steel but copper wire and zinc handles. Scrap processors now are so proficient that virtually 100 percent of the zinc in recycled automobiles is recovered. These skills will have to become even more highly developed, however, if recycling of iron and steel is not going to result in their contamination by other metals.[77]

Market development must be the first priority for recycling's promoters. Promotion would best be accomplished by stimulating investment in electric arc furnaces and removing trade barriers. The need to conserve energy has been the greatest impetus to the use of

"Scrap processors now are so proficient that virtually 100 percent of the zinc in recycled automobiles is recovered."

scrap because scrap contains great quantities of embodied energy. Eliminating subsidies for energy production and use should be a high priority for promoting iron and steel scrap recycling markets.

Promotion of iron and steel collection will be much more difficult. Beverage container deposits help recover steel as well as aluminum and glass, and more important, they virtually eliminate the use of the steel can. This saves resources overall. Substituting more readily recyclable aluminum in food containers might also be encouraged.

Flow control laws—laws requiring that recyclables flow to publicly owned or backed resource recovery facilities—can hurt steel recycling just as much as they hurt paper recycling. Monopolization of municipal markets for scrap collection diminishes the marketability of scrap by reducing economic incentives for scrap collection.

Just as investments in electric arc furnaces and direct reduction of iron ore promote recycling, so too can investments in decreasing the amount of scrap produced in conventional steel making. Most steel is cast by first cooling and then reheating pig iron for casting. In the United States, 21 percent of all steel is continuously cast, compared to 32 and 60 percent in Eastern European countries and Japan.[78] Continuous casting, though requiring large capital investments, will eliminate much of the requirement for reheating and will also eliminate large quantities of the home scrap produced. Continuous casting would thus increase demand for iron ore, directly reduced iron, or obsolete scrap to replace home scrap. Given the large reservoir of obsolete scrap available, application of continuous casting could provide a large opportunity for increasing scrap use.

Norway and Sweden have been praised widely for their efforts to recycle scrap cars. Sweden in the seventies suffered from the blight of 400,000 abandoned car hulks littering the countryside.[79] A Swedish law took effect in 1976 requiring disposal of car hulks with authorized scrap dealers. In Norway, 50,000 hulks similarly had been abandoned, with 20,000 per year being added to this total. Norway followed Sweden's example and enacted its own automobile disposal law, but applied tax rather than regulatory policy. Enacted in May, 1978, Norway's automobile deposit law imposed a $100 deposit on new cars, refundable with a $50 bonus for any car properly disposed. The law resulted in the collection of 33,000 car hulks in the first eight months of the program's operation compared to an average 20,000 per year before the law.[80]

Though Norway's car deposit and Sweden's disposal law have been apparent successes, they would have been unnecessary without artificial constraints on the scrap market. Sweden has essentially prohibited exports of iron and steel scrap since 1927, and Norway permits export of scrap only when the would-be exporter demonstrates that no market for it exists in Norway. The result is a greatly reduced market that permits price fixing and artificially suppressed prices.[81]

On the other hand, Norway produces iron ore, a fact that one would expect to reduce scrap use.[82] The automobile deposit may have helped offset this factor: The refund system reduced the cost of scrap collection and thus encouraged iron and steel recycling. The automobile deposit-refund policy could also be applied to spur recycling in iron ore-rich countries such as Brazil.

Just as the complexity of iron and steel, aluminum, and paper recycling has grown with the variety and sophistication of society's material needs, the matrix of forces affecting recycling rates has grown. Deflecting and concentrating these forces in ways that accelerate recycling has thus become a difficult task. But by applying the lessons learned in materials recycling in the seventies, lessons that clearly define a few basic principles, recycling can serve society's interests as no other process can.

Steps to a "Recycling Society"

When Epimetheus ran out of materials for mankind, Prometheus saved the day by providing energy, the ultimate resource. Society has used energy to create a wealth of machines and shelter. But now as the age of cheap energy fades, and as inflation, joblessness, and pollution intensify, sustaining material living standards in rich countries and satisfying basic material needs in poor countries becomes more difficult than ever. Recycling, in a kind of reversal of the Promethean solution, yields back much of the energy and capital invested in materials. In this way, recycling conserves energy, fights pollution and inflation, creates jobs, and improves the outlook for the future of materials.

Progress made in the seventies proves recycling's practicality and worth. The ability of Japan and the Netherlands to collect half of their waste paper suggests that the world can profitably double its rate of paper recycling. The success of programs encouraging the sorting and recycling of consumer waste in some Japanese cities has reduced the amount of land required for waste dumps by 40 percent, thus saving disposal costs and improving the environment. Beverage container deposit legislation in nine U.S. states has proven the political and economic desirability of recycling. Return rates for bottles and cans exceed 90 percent in these states. Maine has cut its litter collection costs by 60 percent, and Michigan's economy has gained a net total of 4,600 jobs.

The development of a dynamic international trade in scrap paper, aluminum, and iron and steel has shown that huge markets can be created for collected waste. South Korea's ability to produce 40 percent of its paper from *imported* waste paper indicates that paper use can be expanded in increasingly literate Third World societies, without increasing pressure on forests. And because mills for recycling paper cost half as much to build as mills using virgin pulp, recycling can reduce the debts of developing countries. Large imports of aluminum scrap by Italy and Japan have enabled them to sustain industries suffering from the high cost of oil-fired electricity. The United States has sustained a competitive aluminum industry by increasing recycling to the extent that it now produces more aluminum from recycled cans than Africa produces in total.

Spain and Italy have shown that they can compete successfully in steel markets by using purchased iron and steel scrap instead of iron ore for half their production requirements. The United States, with its $1.3 billion annual earnings from exported scrap iron and steel, has illustrated the tangible value of collecting waste.

Nations that have moved toward recycling paper, aluminum, and iron and steel have thus enhanced their competitive position in international markets. Recycling will become an even more important factor in international competitiveness as energy and capital costs increase the cost of producing virgin materials.

Despite gains, the world has fallen far short of achieving recycling's potential. Only about one-fourth of the paper, aluminum, and iron and steel used in the world is recovered for recycling. This rate could be doubled or tripled for each material. But a series of difficult steps must be taken to collect recyclable materials and to develop additional markets for them.

Three steps will lead to a "recycling society." The first requires that consumers pay the full costs of the materials they use. The world's forests have been cut faster than they have been replaced, a practice that makes wood cheaper now, but at the expense of future generations. Setting aside additional forest reserves would make virgin pulpwood more expensive compared to waste paper, and would both assure the protection of some forests and encourage paper companies to buy waste paper. The U.S. Forest Service, which owns half the softwood timber in the United States, should consider reducing sales of trees for harvesting as long as waste paper is underutilized.

This first step also requires a special effort to reduce energy price subsidies. No single factor has increased recycling more in the last 30 years than the energy price increases of the seventies. Recycling saves energy, and industries adopt recycling as a way of cutting energy costs; but when the price paid by industry for energy is distorted by subsidies, industries are less motivated to recycle. Thus, when societies subsidize energy use by providing grants or loans for dams and

"No single factor has increased recycling more in the last 30 years than the energy price increases of the seventies."

power plants, or by applying measures that hold the price of energy below replacement costs, they encourage environmental degradation. To subsidize energy consumption is to subsidize the "throw-away society."

The second step requires building world markets for scrap paper, aluminum, and iron and steel. Wealthy countries restrain the export of scrap iron and steel and seriously inhibit the use of imported scrap in developing countries. The Common Market countries restrict scrap trade between a member country and a nonmember country. Denmark, Sweden, and Austria prohibit essentially all scrap exports, and the United States continually considers limiting scrap exports. Few countries needing new steel production capacity will risk reliance on imported scrap unless scrap-exporting countries remove the threat of scrap "embargoes."

The final step, one that will also reduce environmental subsidies, promote international scrap trade, and soften the impact of higher energy prices, is the greater collection of wastes. Container deposit legislation can dramatically increase the return of beverage containers. Incentives, information, or the threat of fines and noncollection of garbage can induce greater collection of recyclable material. A wide variety of policies, in fact, will stimulate recycling, and can be applied on national or local levels.

These steps will not be taken simply because they are logical or urgently needed, but because concerned citizens insist that they be taken. Conservationists have shown too little interest in assuring market pricing for energy and free trade of scrap materials, though they have much at stake in these policies. National and local government leaders have shown little willingness to take the difficult step of requiring collection of recyclable materials, but the rising costs of litter cleanup and landfilling waste will increasingly press them to do so. Industry leaders will increasingly be forced by higher energy and raw materials prices to consider recycling or face a future in which they cannot compete.

The future of all society will be an uneasy one if a major portion of the world is forced to live with a low or declining materials standard. As physicist David Rose has written, "In the worldwide search for routes to a juster and more sustainable society it has become clear that a peace in which the world is divided ever more rigorously into haves and have-nots is neither just nor likely to be sustainable."[83] Materials recycling has become necessary if society is simply to maintain current living standards. But within this necessity lies the opportunity to improve the material well-being of all the world's people, and to do so without great cost to the environment. In this resides the great virtue of recycling.

Notes

1. Thomas Bulfinch, *Bulfinch's Mythology* (London: Spring Books, 1969), p. 14.

2. William T. Keeton, Biological Science (New York: W.W. Norton & Co., 1967), p. 154.

3. H.E. Goeller and A.M. Weinberg, "The Age of Substitutability," *Science,* February 20, 1976, p. 685.

4. See John H. Gibbons and William U. Chandler, *Energy: The Conservation Revolution* (New York: Plenum Publishing Company, 1981).

5. This analogy was first suggested by energy educator John Yegge, formerly of Oak Ridge Associated Universities, Oak Ridge, Tennessee.

6. William E. Franklin, Marjorie Franklin, and Robert Hunt, *Waste Paper: The Future of a Resource* (New York: Franklin Associates and the American Paper Institute, 1982), p. 9.

7. Renaud de la Taille, "Pas de civilisation industrielle sans les metaux exotiques," *Science & Vie,* June, 1983, pp. 98-164.

8. *Recycled Metals in the 1980's* (New York: National Association of Recycling Industries, 1982), pp. 99-117.

9. Goeller and Weinberg, "The Age of Substitutability."

10. Some controversy exists regarding the carcinogenicity of benzopyrene.

11. Derived from R.C. Ziegler et al., "Environmental Impacts of Virgin and Recycled Steel and Aluminum" (Springfield, Va.: National Technical Information Service, 1976).

12. U.S. Congress Office of Technology Assessment, *Wood Use* (Washington, D.C.: U.S. Government Printing Office, August 1983), p. 50.

13. See the section "Wood and Plant Materials," *Science,* February 21, 1976, pp. 747-773; *Renewable Resources for Industrial Materials* (Washington, D.C.: National Academy of Sciences, 1976), p. 243; Sandra Postel, "Sustaining Forests," Lester Brown, ed., *Worldwatch Progress Report, 1984* (New York: W.W. Norton, forthcoming); Edgar Gaertner, "La Mort de la Foret," *Le Monde Diplomatique,* August 1983, p. 32.

14. Marion Clawson, *The Economics of U.S. Nonindustrial Private Forests* (Washington, D.C.: Resources For the Future, 1979), pp. 111, 152, 186.

15. Thomas E. Ricks, "Timber Firms Moving to the South As Supplies in Northwest Diminish," *Wall Street Journal,* August 19, 1983.

16. Franklin et al., *Waste Paper: The Future of a Resource,* p. 139.

17. J. Rodney Edwards, American Paper Institute, New York, private communication, June 1983.

18. U.N. Food and Agriculture Organization, Committee on Pulp and Paper, *Waste Paper Data 1978-80* (Rome: May 25-27, 1981 and April 1981).

19. Lester R. Brown, *Building A Sustainable Society* (New York: W.W. Norton & Co., 1981), p. 181.

20. Richard Hertzberg, "NARI's Look at State and Local Recycling Laws," *Resource Recycling,* November/December 1982, pp. 8-10. This article reports an interview with NARI Vice President Ronald Rosenson.

21. *Economic Instruments in Solid Waste Management* (Paris: Organisation for for Economic Co-operation and Development, 1981), pp. 36-37.

22. *Saikuru No Chishiki* (Tokyo: The Clean Japan Center, 1983), pp. 40-41.

23. Ibid.

24. Geoffrey Murray, "Putting 220 Tons of Garbage A Day Where It Belongs," *The Christian Science Monitor,* March 10, 1983.

25. *Waste Paper Recovery* (Paris: Organisation for Economic Co-operation and Development, 1979), pp. 88-116.

26. *Economic Instruments in Solid Waste Management,* pp. 36-37.

27. Janet Marinelli, "Recyclings Little Victories," *Environmental Action,* April 1982, pp. 17-18.

28. Richard Hertzberg, "Islip, New York: Where Mandatory Recycling Works," *Resource Recycling,* May/June, 1983, p. 17.

29. Elizabeth Gallagher, Assistant to the Commissioner of Environmental Control, Town of Islip, New York, private communication, August 12, 1983.

30. *Economic Instruments in Solid Waste Management,* p. 34; *Economic Instruments in Solid Waste Management,* p. 36.

31. *World Environment Report,* January 30, 1982, p. 7.

32. *Waste Paper Data,* pp. 1-6; and Franklin et al., *Waster Paper: The Future of a Resource,* pp. 139-147. The value of waste paper trade is estimated by using actual unpublished American Paper Institute data for U.S. exports and assuming that 40 percent of gross world trade in waste paper is American.

33. See Franklin et al., *Waste Paper: The Future of a Resource,* Appendix G, pp. 138-157.

34. Ibid.

35. John M. Bradley, "Cairo's Garbage Collectors Get Big World Bank Loan," *World Environment Report,* September 30, 1982, pp. 1-2; World Bank press release, Washington, D.C., May 22, 1980.

36. Congressman Ron Wyden (D-Oregon), "Use of Recovered Materials By Federal Agencies," fact sheet (May 10, 1983) describing H.R. 2867, amending the Resource Conservation and Recovery Act of 1976, 90 STAT. 2795; and private communication with Daniel Saltzman, Legislative Assistant to Congressman Wyden, Washington, August 12, 1983; "Recycling's Little Victories," p. 19.

37. Mary Lou Van Deventer, "Whatever Happened To Recycling?," *Not Man Apart,* January 1983.

38. U.S. Congress Office of Technology Assessment, *Industrial Energy Use* (Washington, D.C.: U.S. Government Printing Office, June 1983), p. 71.

39. Celso Furtado, "Dette exterieur: quel type de renegociation?", *Le Monde Diplomatique,* August 1983, p. 16.

40. *Aluminum Statistical Review for 1981* (Washington, D.C.: The Aluminum Association, Inc., 1982), pp. 42-62.

41. Ibid.

42. See William U. Chandler, *The Myth of TVA: 1933-1983* (Cambridge, Mass: Ballinger Publishing Co., October 1983).

43. *Aluminum Statistical Review for 1981*, pp. 22-23.

44. *Aluminum Statistical Review for 1981*, p. 30, and *Minerals Yearbook, 1981, Volume I*, p. 76.

45. *Aluminum Statistical Review for 1981*, p. 44.

46. Brown, *Building A Sustainable Society*, pp. 220, 222.

47. *Minerals Yearbook, 1981, Volume III*, p. 753.

48. David Solomon, "Dam blocked in Australia's hottest environmental dispute," *Christian Science Monitor*, July 6, 1983.

49. *Aluminum Statistical Review for 1981*, p. 44.

50. *Minerals Yearbook, 1981, Volume III*, pp. 557-559.

51. Ibid, p. 559.

52. Al Trumer, "Italy Set To Abandon Its Aluminum Industry," *Journal of Commerce*, July 21, 1982, and "Italian Ministry Grants Aid to Aluminum Industry," *Journal of Commerce*, August 6, 1982.

53. Sumer C. Aggarwal, "Managing Material Shortages: The Russian Way," *Columbia Journal of World Business*, Fall 1980, pp. 26-37.

54. *Aluminum Statistical Review for 1981*, and *Minerals Yearbook, 1981, Volume III*.

55. This was the price of "old cast scrap" in April 1983. This price is down from 43 cents in June of 1979. *Aluminum Smelters: Europe, Japan, USA* (London: Organization of European Aluminum Smelters, April 1983), p. 26.

56. *Aluminum Smelters*, p. 10.

57. *Aluminum Statistical Review for 1981*, p. 47.

58. "Reverse Vending Machines," *Resource Recycling*, November/December 1982, pp. 18-20.

59. "Aluminum Recovery? Can Do!", *Sweden Now*, February 1982, p. 36.

60. "Community Recycling Update," *Resource Recycling*, November/December 1982, p. 3.

61. See William K. Shireman et al., *Can and Bottle Bills: The CalPIRG-ELS Study Group Report* (Stanford, Calif.: California Public Interest Research Group and the Standford Environmental Law Society, 1981), pp. v-vii; and "States Experience with Beverage Container Deposit Laws Shows Positive Benefits," U.S. Congress General Accounting Office, December 11, 1980, pp. 52-53.

62. Ibid.

63. "Is Recycling the Tin Can a Can of Worms?", *Phoenix Quarterly, Journal of the Institute of Scrap Iron and Steel,* Spring 1977.

64. Reported by Frank X. McCawley, physical scientist, Division of Nonferrous Metals, U.S. Bureau of Mines, private communication, July 14, 1983.

65. Shireman, *Can and Bottle Bills,* pp. B-1, B-2.

66. This was the central purpose of the "World Aluminum Industry Study" as explained by Alfredo Dammert, a principal researcher, World Bank, Washington, private communication, August 11, 1983.

67. *Shoe,* Tribune Company Syndicate, Inc., as reprinted in *Resource Recycling,* May/June 1983, p. 35.

68. *Recycled Metals in the 1980's* (New York: National Association of Recycling Industries, 1982), p. 90.

69. *Facts, 1981 Yearbook of the Institute of the Institute of Scrap Iron and Steel, Inc.,* 39th ed. (Washington, D.C.: 1982), p. 3.

70. U.S. Congress Office of Technology Assessment, *Technology and Steel Industry Competitiveness* (Washington, D.C.: U.S. Government Printing Office, June 1980), p. 204; and *Industrial Energy Use,* p. 144.

71. Derived from the *Minerals Yearbook, 1981, Volume III.*

72. This figure represents automotive scrap as a percentage of all iron and steel products scrapped (i.e., "becoming obsolescent") in the United States in the period of a year, according to an estimate for 1974 in U.S. Congress Office of Technology Assessment, *Technical Options for Conservation of Metals: Case Studies of Selected Metals and Products* (Washington, D.C.: U.S. Government Printing Office, September 1979), p. 26.

73. "Near-Record 21 Million Tons of Ferrous Discards Added to Scrap Backlog in 1981," *Phoenix Quarterly,* Winter 1983, pp. 6-8; and Denis Hayes,

"Repairs, Reuse, Recycling—First Steps Toward a Sustainable Society" (Washington, D.C.: Worldwatch Institute, September 1978), p. 17.

74. Donald Barnett, World Bank, private communcation, July 14, 1983; *Minerals Yearbook, 1981, Volume III,* pp. 740-741.

75. *Minerals Yearbook, 1981, Volume I,* p. 488.

76. *Technology and Steel Industry Competitiveness,* pp. 58-69.

77. "Zinc Die Cast--Autos Are Using Less, But Shredders Are Recovering More," *Phoenix Quarterly,* Winter 1983, p. 8; Leslie R. Parkes, "Metals Face an Uncertain Future," *New Scientist,* July 14, 1983, p. 93; and Herschel Cutler, executive director, Institute of Scrap Iron and Steel, private communication, August 11, 1983.

78. *Industrial Energy Use,* p. 155.

79. C.L. Astedt, "Recovery of Car Hulks in Sweden," in *Economic Instruments in Solid Waste Management,* pp. 89-107.

80. J. Thompson, "The Recovery of Car Hulks in Norway," in *Economic Instruments in Solid Waste Management,* pp. 109-125.

81. Thompson, "The Recovery of Car Hulks in Norway," p. 112; C. L. Astedt, "The Recovery of Car Hulks in Sweden," pp. 91-92.

82. William T. Hogan, *World Steel in the 1980s: A Case of Survival* (Lexington, Mass.: Lexington Books, 1983), p. 52.

83. D.J. Rose and R. K. Lester, "Nuclear Power, Nuclear Weapons, and International Stability," *Scientific American,* New York, May 1978, p. 57.

WILLIAM U. CHANDLER is a Senior Researcher at Worldwatch Institute in Washington, D.C. He is co-author of *Energy: The Conservation Revolution* and author of *The Myth of TVA,* as well as many articles on energy and the environment.

THE WORLDWATCH PAPER SERIES

No. of Copies

______ 1. **The Other Energy Crisis: Firewood** by Erik Eckholm.
______ 2. **The Politics and Responsibility of the North American Breadbasket** by Lester R. Brown.
______ 3. **Women in Politics: A Global Review** by Kathleen Newland.
______ 4. **Energy: The Case for Conservation** by Denis Hayes.
______ 5. **Twenty-two Dimensions of the Population Problem** by Lester R. Brown, Patricia L. McGrath, and Bruce Stokes.
______ 6. **Nuclear Power: The Fifth Horseman** by Denis Hayes.
______ 7. **The Unfinished Assignment: Equal Education for Women** by Patricia L. McGrath.
______ 8. **World Population Trends: Signs of Hope, Signs of Stress** by Lester R. Brown.
______ 9. **The Two Faces of Malnutrition** by Erik Eckholm and Frank Record.
______ 10. **Health: The Family Planning Factor** by Erik Eckholm and Kathleen Newland.
______ 11. **Energy: The Solar Prospect** by Denis Hayes.
______ 12. **Filling The Family Planning Gap** by Bruce Stokes.
______ 13. **Spreading Deserts—The Hand of Man** by Erik Eckholm and Lester R. Brown.
______ 14. **Redefining National Security** by Lester R. Brown.
______ 15. **Energy for Development: Third World Options** by Denis Hayes.
______ 16. **Women and Population Growth: Choice Beyond Childbearing** by Kathleen Newland.
______ 17. **Local Responses to Global Problems: A Key to Meeting Basic Human Needs** by Bruce Stokes.
______ 18. **Cutting Tobacco's Toll** by Erik Eckholm.
______ 19. **The Solar Energy Timetable** by Denis Hayes.
______ 20. **The Global Economic Prospect: New Sources of Economic Stress** by Lester R. Brown.
______ 21. **Soft Technologies, Hard Choices** by Colin Norman.
______ 22. **Disappearing Species: The Social Challenge** by Erik Eckholm.
______ 23. **Repairs, Reuse, Recycling—First Steps Toward a Sustainable Society** by Denis Hayes.
______ 24. **The Worldwide Loss of Cropland** by Lester R. Brown.
______ 25. **Worker Participation—Productivity and the Quality of Work Life** by Bruce Stokes.
______ 26. **Planting for the Future: Forestry for Human Needs** by Erik Eckholm.
______ 27. **Pollution: The Neglected Dimensions** by Denis Hayes.
______ 28. **Global Employment and Economic Justice: The Policy Challenge** by Kathleen Newland.
______ 29. **Resource Trends and Population Policy: A Time for Reassessment** by Lester R. Brown.
______ 30. **The Dispossessed of the Earth: Land Reform and Sustainable Development** by Erik Eckholm.
______ 31. **Knowledge and Power: The Global Research and Development Budget** by Colin Norman.
______ 32. **The Future of the Automobile in an Oil-Short World** by Lester R. Brown, Christopher Flavin, and Colin Norman.
______ 33. **International Migration: The Search for Work** by Kathleen Newland.
______ 34. **Inflation: The Rising Cost of Living on a Small Planet** by Robert Fuller.
______ 35. **Food or Fuel: New Competition for the World's Cropland** by Lester R. Brown.
______ 36. **The Future of Synthetic Materials: The Petroleum Connection** by Christopher Flavin.
______ 37. **Women, Men, and The Division of Labor** by Kathleen Newland.

_____ 38. **City Limits: Emerging Constraints on Urban Growth** by Kathleen Newland.

_____ 39. **Microelectronics at Work: Productivity and Jobs in the World Economy** by Colin Norman.

_____ 40. **Energy and Architecture: The Solar and Conservation Potential** by Christopher Flavin.

_____ 41. **Men and Family Planning** by Bruce Stokes.

_____ 42. **Wood: An Ancient Fuel with a New Future** by Nigel Smith.

_____ 43. **Refugees: The New International Politics of Displacement** by Kathleen Newland.

_____ 44. **Rivers of Energy: The Hydropower Potential** by Daniel Deudney.

_____ 45. **Wind Power: A Turning Point** by Christopher Flavin.

_____ 46. **Global Housing Prospects: The Resource Constraints** by Bruce Stokes.

_____ 47. **Infant Mortality and the Health of Societies** by Kathleen Newland.

_____ 48. **Six Steps to a Sustainable Society** by Lester R. Brown and Pamela Shaw.

_____ 49. **Productivity: The New Economic Context** by Kathleen Newland.

_____ 50. **Space: The High Frontier in Perspective** by Daniel Deudney.

_____ 51. **U.S. and Soviet Agriculture: The Shifting Balance of Power** by Lester R. Brown.

_____ 52. **Electricity from Sunlight: The Future of Photovoltaics** by Christopher Flavin.

_____ 53. **Population Policies for a New Economic Era** by Lester R. Brown.

_____ 54. **Promoting Population Stabilization: Incentives for Small Families** by Judith Jacobsen

_____ 55. **Whole Earth Security: A Geopolitics of Peace** by Daniel Deudney

_____ 56. **Materials Recycling: The Virtue of Necessity** by William U. Chandler

_____ **Total Copies**

Single Copy—$2.00

Bulk Copies (any combination of titles)
2-10: $1.50 each 11-50: $1.25 each 51 or more: $1.00 each

Calendar Year Subscription (1983 subscription begins with Paper 53)
$25.00 _____

Make check payable to Worldwatch Institute
1776 Massachusetts Avenue NW, Washington, D.C. 20036 USA

Enclosed is my check for U.S. $ _____

____
name

____
address

____
city **state** **zip/country**